OFFICIAL ANNUAL

CW01582209

GET TO KNOW ...
ZANE

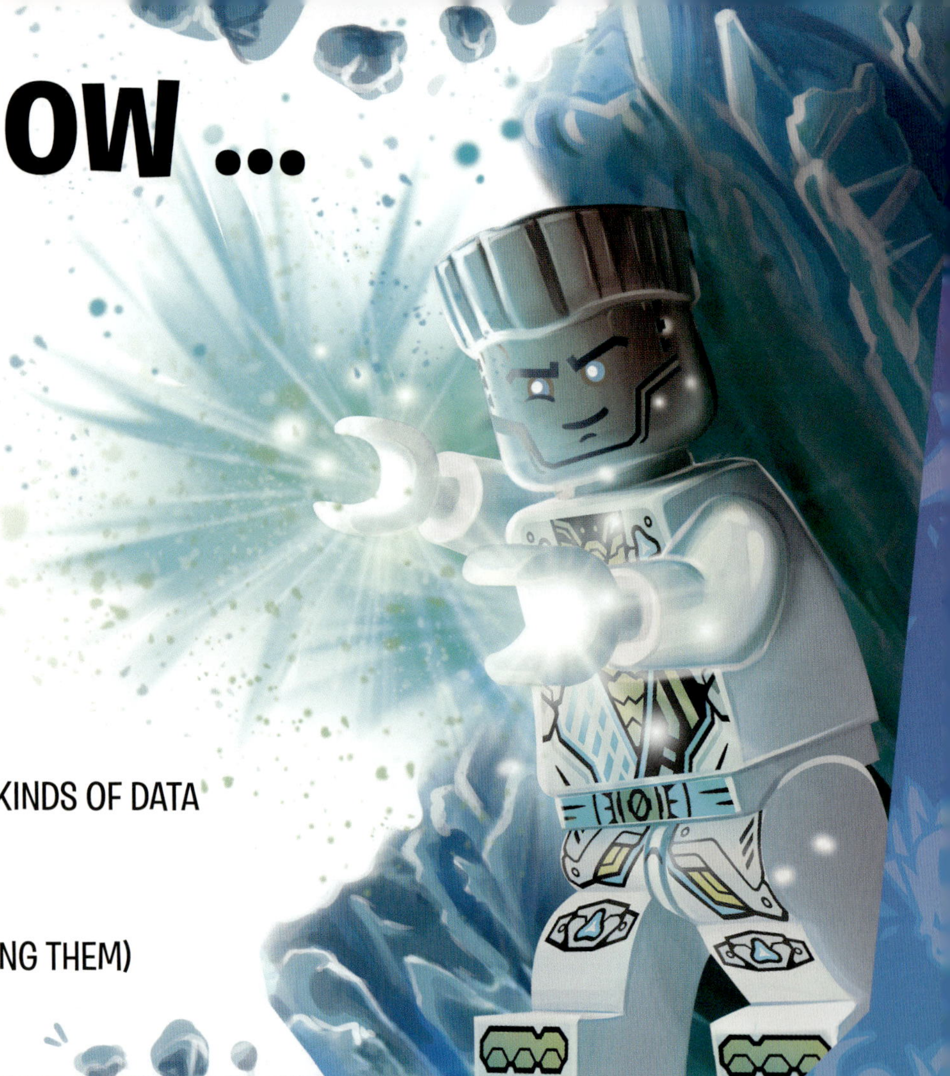

PROFESSION:
QUIET AND MYSTERIOUS

SKILLS:
ELEMENTAL MASTER OF ICE

INTERESTS:
COLLECTING AND ANALYZING ALL KINDS OF DATA

BIGGEST CHALLENGE:
UNDERSTANDING JOKES (OR TELLING THEM)

Zane was found by Kai and Nya in a techno-cocoon years after the Merge. He couldn't remember what happened on the day the Merge started.

While the ninja searched for the Dragon Cores, Zane remained in the Monastery of Spinjitzu. He was busy collecting data about mysterious portals and ... the habits of Mr Frohicky.

During a mission to a monastery in the First Realm, Zane unexpectedly met the person he missed the most – Pixal.

The attack of the dragon hunters was met with an icy response from Zane. Mark two fragments that do not match the scene.

The enemy caught Zane off guard! Quick! Connect the dots to reveal the weapon the warrior has so Zane knows how to defend himself!

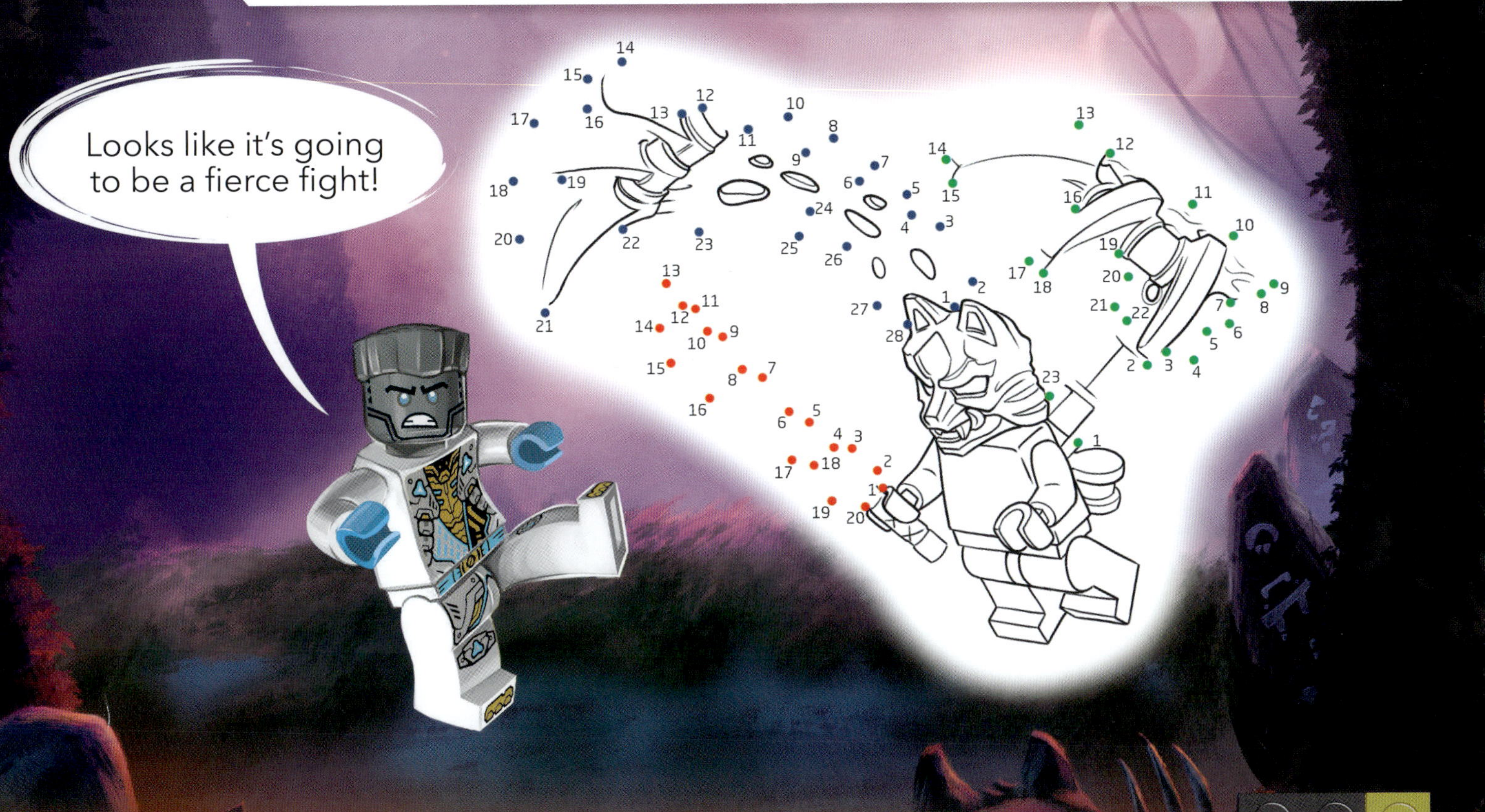

Look closely at Zane's Ice Glider. Find the set that contains some of the parts from the Glider.

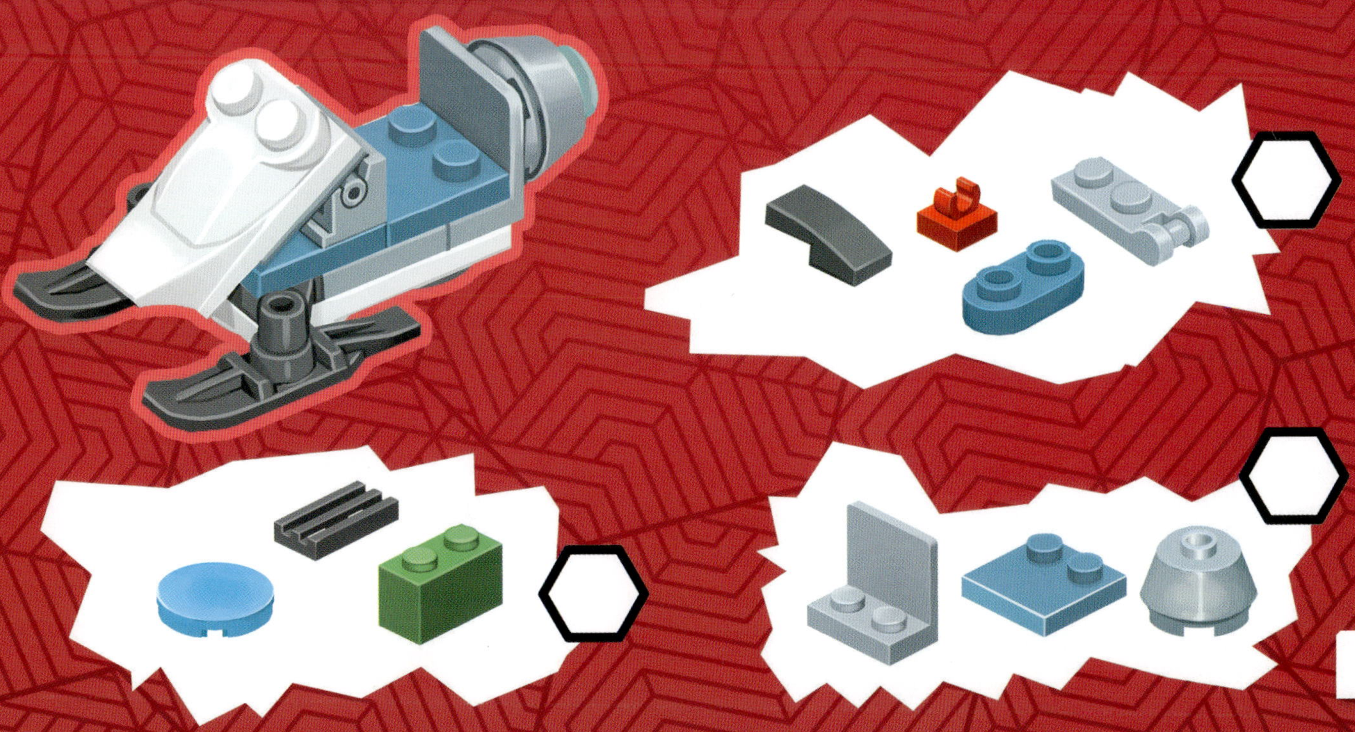

The ninja team's mission is to protect the Source Dragons from danger. Study the picture of the Source Dragon of Motion and mark one square from each set that matches the dragon.

Which of these characters is the true spirit of the temple?
To find out, spot the one that is different from the others.

Find the path that will lead Zane to his vehicle.

A BIGGER MESS

A few minutes later ...
Done. But according to my calculations, the ice is going to –
Don't you worry about anything! Thank you!
Finally, a day without cleaning!
Next morning ...
Hmm ...
Oh, Zane! You're not gonna believe what happened ...
I tried to warn you.

Sound the alarm! Someone is trying to crack the database security codes. Select the correct pattern, and connect the elements to lock the system.

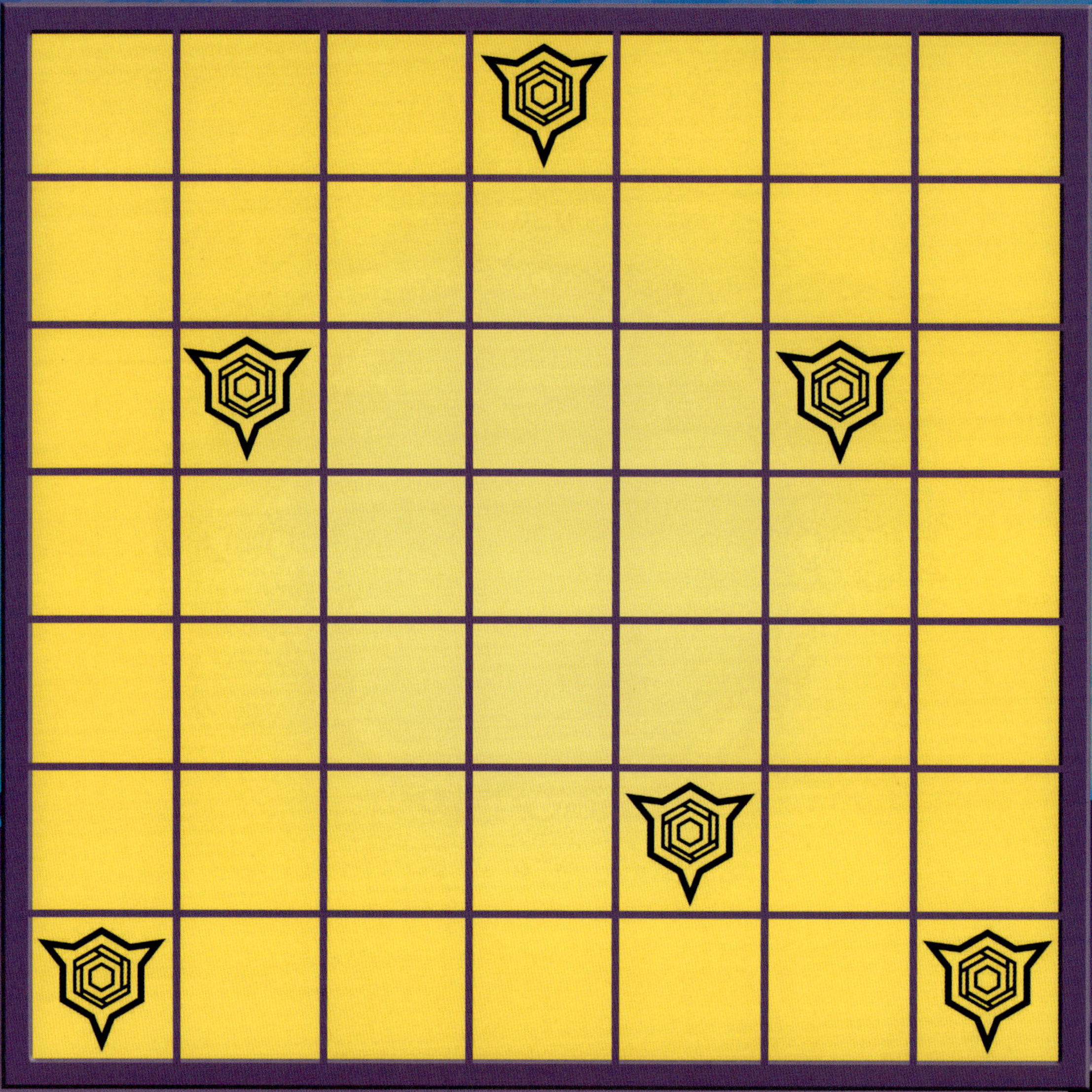

A magic spell has changed Zane's size. Number the portraits from the smallest to the largest by writing the correct numbers in the empty boxes. The first one has been done for you.

Follow the code to colour this picture and reveal the droid that is spying on Zane.

Go through the maze and find Zane's Battle Suit Mech. Move in the direction of the arrows. You can only land on rocks covered in snow. Watch out for enemies!

AN IMPORTANT NOTE

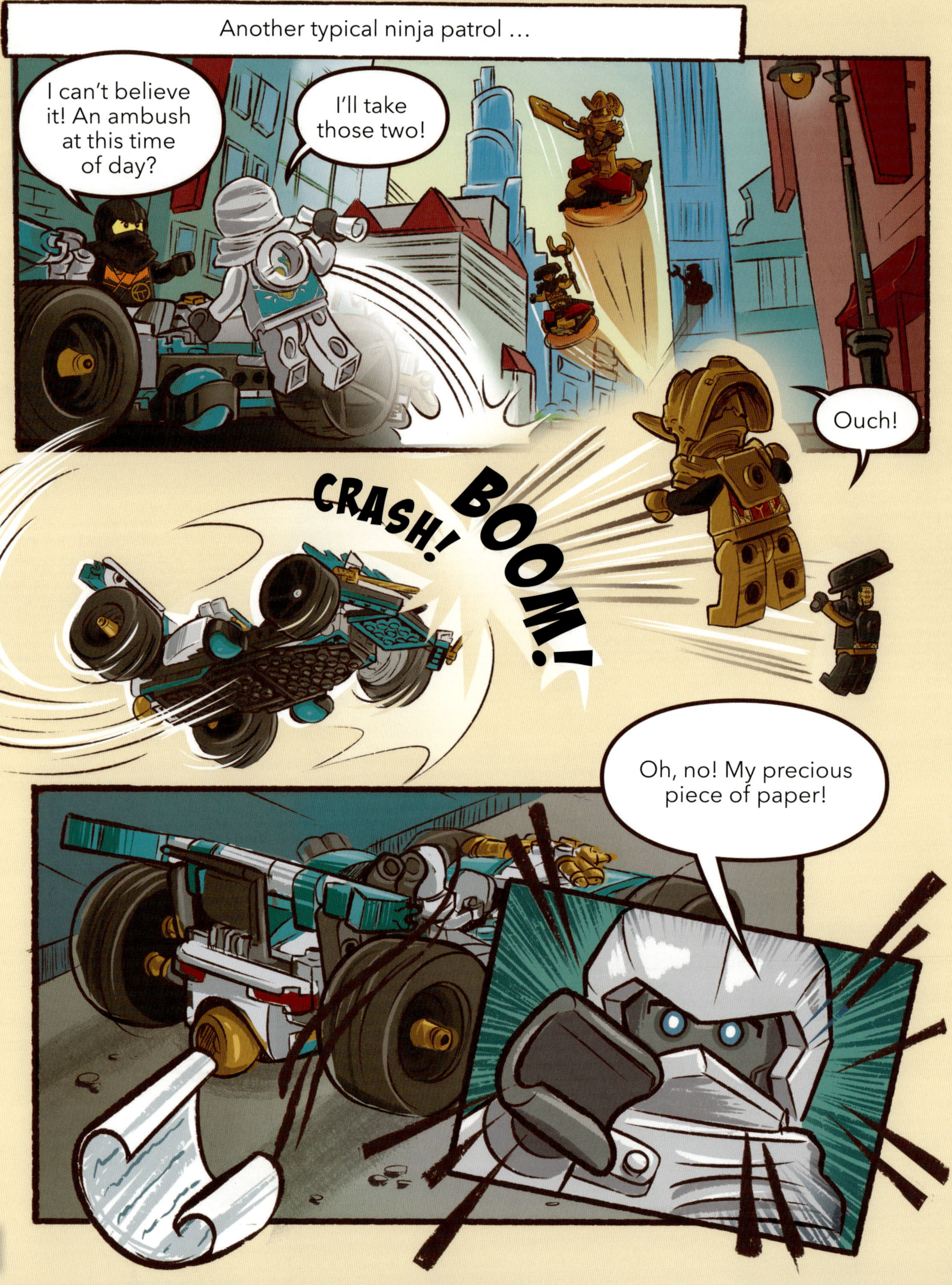

Don't you touch that!
?!
I've warned you!
Phew! Got it! I feared I was going to lose it!
Really? Why's this note so important?
I wrote a poem for Pixal. I didn't want anyone to read it …
Besides, it's not finished … See? The rhymes aren't perfect yet.
Um … I think Pixal's gonna love it.

Zane is searching for Arin. Circle five differences between the two pictures of Zane riding his Ice Motorcycle.

Follow the colour code to match the warriors to their weapons.

Zane prepares a catalogue for parts to build new mechs. Draw lines to divide the pieces into four equal groups.

ZANE'S AMAZING POWERS

Zane's Nindroid body has some surprising features, including playing music. Whatever he plays, he always does the robot dance!

Zane can lower the temperature to freeze objects or enemies. He makes Mr Frohicky happy by making ice cubes just for him.

Zane can analyze the potential outcome of each fight in 12,856 ways. When his opponents learn their odds of winning are zero, they don't even try to fight him!

Zane is able to project holographic pictures from his eyes. Who needs a cinema when you have Zane?

Zane's head is able to fully rotate. This means he can keep his eyes on what is happening around him all the time ... until he feels dizzy!

Zane often creates amazing things out of ice, such as long, winding ice tracks. Being the Ice Ninja, he doesn't feel cold, so he can ride his Ice Glider for hours!

Help Zane reach Arin. Follow the trail of Arin's portraits and lead the Titanium Ninja to his destination.

How many of Zane's swords can you count? Write the total in the box below.

Can you help Zane find eight shurikens? Looks like they might come in handy!

It's always great to work together. Look at the ninja team and write the letter of the missing person in each row.

Zane wants to install a turbo boost program. Help him with the installation by connecting the wires into one line from start to finish.

The opponent whose portrait is repeated the most is the one who will fight the Titanium Ninja. Find who it is, so Zane can prepare for battle.

Zane is getting ready for his next mission. Make sure his uniform is correct. Can you find one difference on each portrait of Zane?

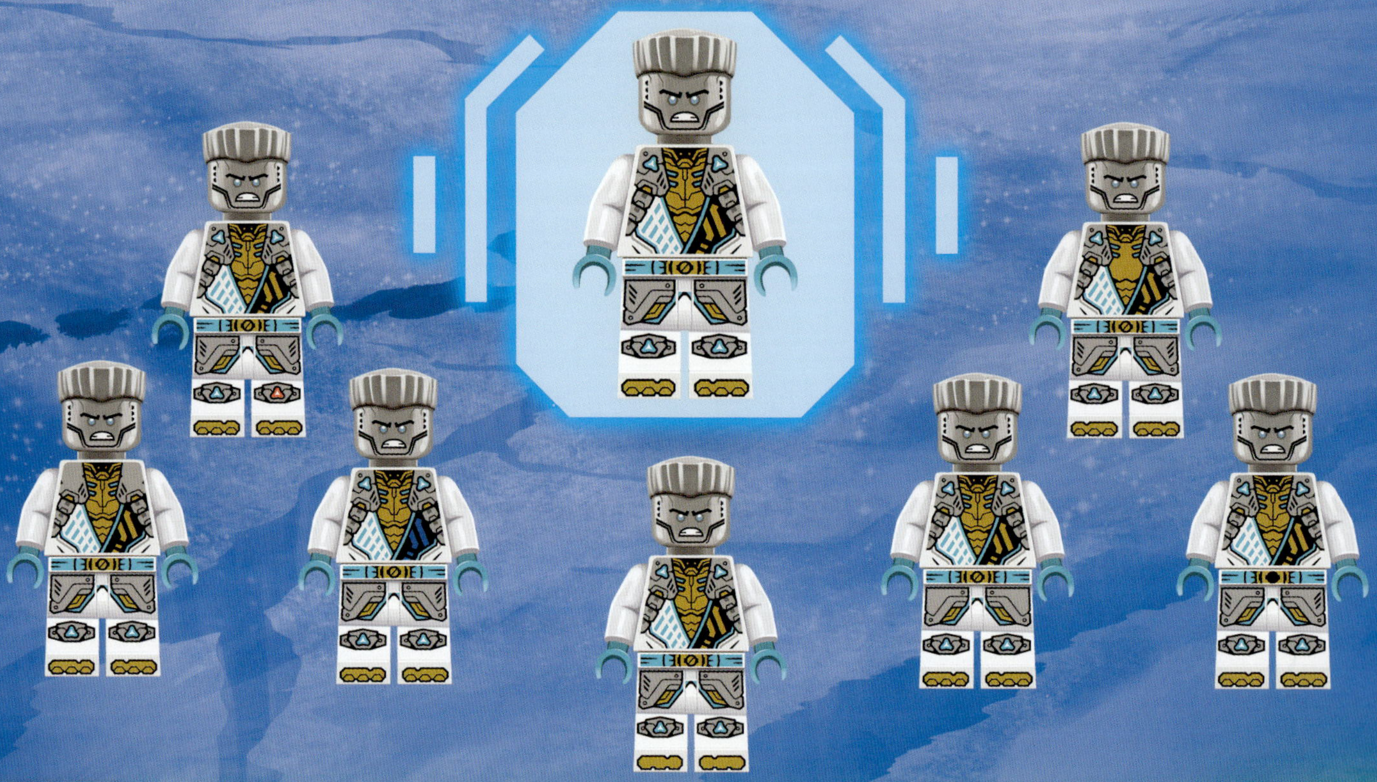

During intensive training, sometimes even shadows can't keep up with ninjas! Match each ninja to their shadow by writing the correct letters in the boxes.

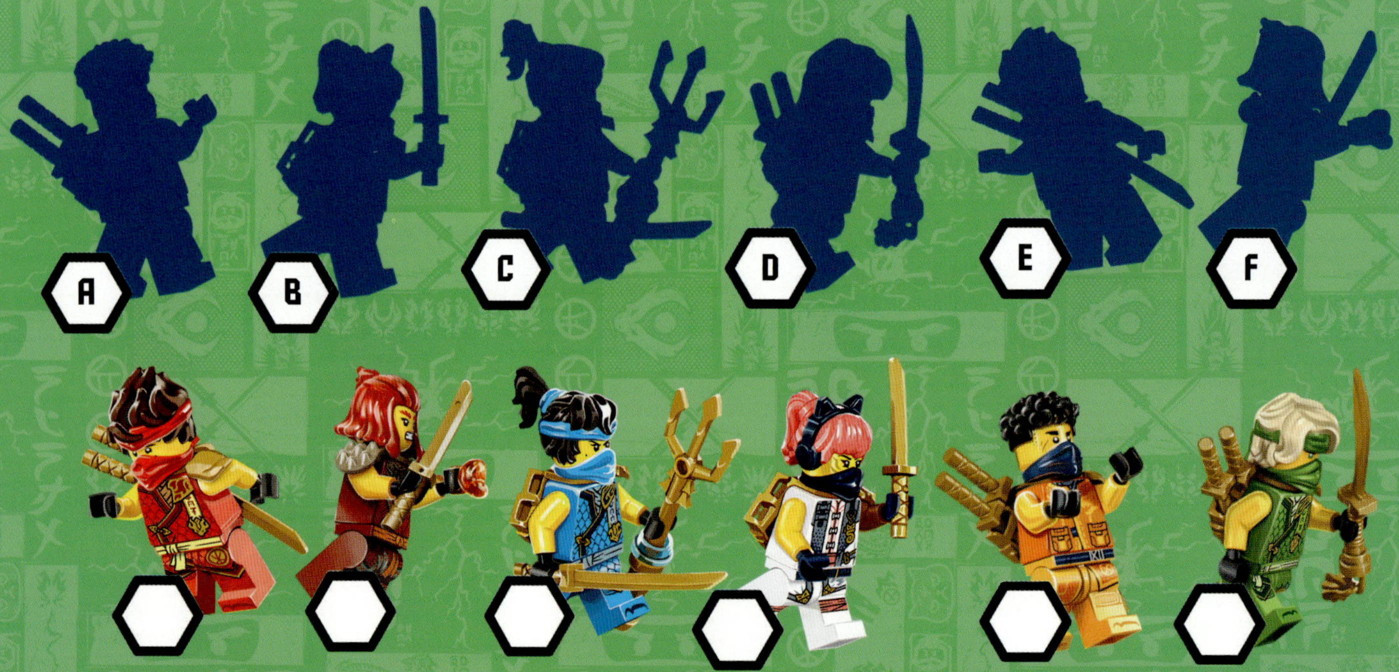

Who is standing in Zane's way today? Draw a villain in the empty space below.

Follow the example and draw Zane's facial expressions to match each of the descriptions below.

Mr Frohicky surprised Zane and gave him … a Mr Frohicky mascot. Put the picture pieces in the correct order by writing the numbers in the empty boxes.

Zane is in a hurry to meet someone. To find out who it is, follow the pattern of arrows in the box at the top.

Thanks to Rontu and Egalt, Zane knows the Rising Dragon Technique. Look at the training scene below and work out where to put each puzzle piece to complete the picture.

You've reached the end of this cool adventure! Answer these questions to find out how well you know Zane.

1. Zane has been known as:
   a) The Concrete Ninja
   b) The Titanium Ninja
   c) The Golden Ninja

2. Being a Nindroid, Zane is not able to:
   a) Play songs
   b) Spin his head
   c) Shoot fireballs

3. When the ninja went to look for the Dragon Cores, Zane stayed at the monastery with:
   a) 
   b) 
   c) 

4. Zane wrote a special poem for:
   a) Pixal
   b) Sora
   c) No one

5. Who did Zane go looking for?
   a) Lloyd
   b) Arin
   c) Nya

GET TO KNOW ...
JUST JASON

PROFESSION:
CONTENT CREATOR

FAVORITE GADGET:
SKATEBOARD

LIKES:
EXTREME SPORTS, STUNTS, COLD PIZZA

DOESN'T LIKE:
HOT PIZZA

Just Jason is a part of the No Limits Crew. Together with the rest of the team, he has a very popular channel where he shares his *extreme* passions.

His videos are for viewers with nerves of steel! They are full of epic tricks, speed and sometimes even explosions.

Jason's middle name is Courage. He isn't afraid of anything – not even selfies with sharks!

Ready for a new super-extreme trick? Help Jason get ready by colouring in the drawing that is identical to the picture below.

A

B

C

D

Oops, someone was late for the city tour.
Read the clues and find out who it was.

This person:

- is an adult
- doesn't wear a hat
- has a zipped sweatshirt
- has straight hair

Time for a giant water slalom challenge! Take Jason on the path that has the most sharks!

TEST DRIVE

Colour me!

"Hi! Today I'm at Mech Max's garage," said Just Jason, as he started recording a video for his channel. "I'm about to find out which of her wild designs you've chosen for my extreme testing," he explained to his viewers.

"A hospital bed, a hot dog on four wheels or a rolling toilet seat? Let's see which ride got the most votes," he said as he looked at the results.

"You gotta be kidding!" he exclaimed, surprised by the choice.

"The Ultimate Extreme Tester (me) is gonna be testing a not-so-extreme ... rolling toilet," he announced. Then he hopped into his ride and drove off, ready for the challenge.

"Whoa!" he shouted, as he saw a roaring car speeding straight at him, with a notorious crook behind its wheel.

The tires screeched and the car stopped. The crook looked at Just Jason and burst out laughing.

"What?! A dude in a big toilet?! In the middle of the street? AH HA HA HA!"

She was laughing so hard that she didn't see Just Jason using his plunger to intercept the diamond she had stolen, or the police pull up to take her away.

"I guess a rolling toilet test drive can be pretty extreme, after all!" he concluded.

Just Jason loooves doughnuts! Take him to the doughnut truck as fast as possible.

Mech Max created another awesome vehicle! Connect the dots to see her new creation.

Who scored the most points in this arcade game? To find out, spot the player standing in front of the machine that is different from the others.

Lunch break! Look at Jason's burger and mark the correct set of ingredients.

Jason will try to stay on his skateboard for 24 hours! Find out who will be filming his stunt by working out which picture completes the scene.

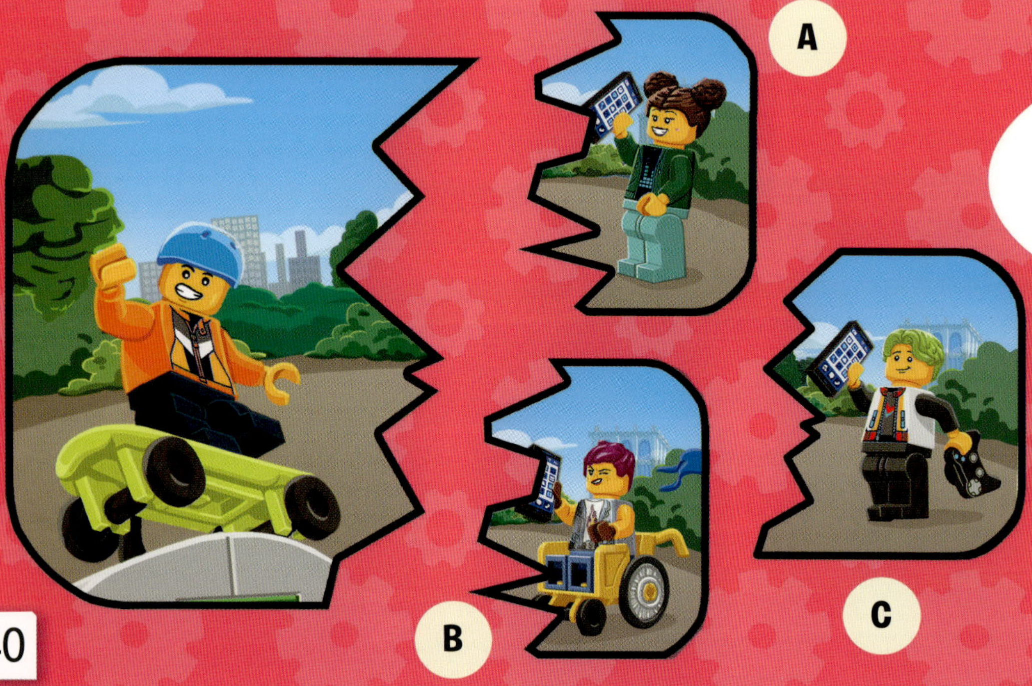

The garage is a busy place today! See if you can spot 10 differences between the pictures.

Just Jason is a great driver but even he can't drive four cars at once! Untangle the lines to discover who will drive each vehicle.

Welcome to the No Limits Crew fan meeting! Look at the fans and match them to the zoomed-in images.

As an amateur stuntman, Jason practices epic tricks. Look at the tricks below and work out the sequence, writing the missing number in each blank space.

The city bus is ready for tours. Mark one image in each section that matches the bus.

Which skateboard does Jason like most from his collection? To find out, circle the skateboard that is not covered by the others.

There's a lot going on at the seaside harbour today!
Can you help Jason find all the items shown in the box?

TOO EPIC!
What's up, viewers? Check out my brand new stunt!
First, the slalom! Ha ha!
And now the epic jump! Woohoo!
It's time for the blood-curdling part!
Yikes!

I'm flying! Oh, yeah!
And the grand finale …
Double chocolate, please!
Let's check how many likes I have.
Zero?!
Sorry …
… I was watching your epic stunt and forgot to press record.
No problem, bro. We'll do it again!
Just maybe without the seagull part!

Just Jason is filming the big race around the city.
Look at his report and circle the details that make the smaller pictures different from the big one.

Can you work out who won the race? The driver who doesn't have a matching outline was the winner.

It was an awesome ride! Number the ramps from smallest to largest to find Jason's epic route.

These are the No Limits Crew's favourite gadgets. Divide them into four groups, each containing one of every item.

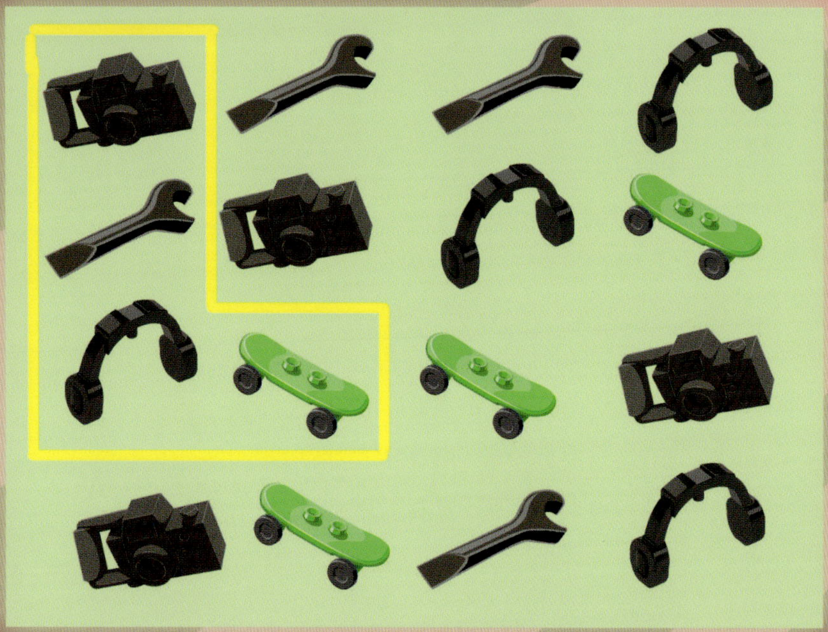

For his next challenge, Jason is a lifeguard. Help build his vehicle by writing the correct number in each blank space.

Just Jason is lightning fast! See for yourself and choose the puzzle pieces that will make Jason disappear.

Parkour in a scrapyard? Why not! Study the picture fragments and work out which ones appear in the main image.

When riding a skateboard, Jason never forgets his helmet! Find the shadows that exactly match the pictures of Jason.

Just Jason is ready for a new challenge! Design a ramp for him using the items shown in the box.

PERFECT SELFIE

Hi, Rocket Racer! Can I get a selfie?
Sure, buddy!
Do I smell onions?
That's possible. I just ate the triple onion burger. Say cheese!
I hate cheese … I mean onion! BLEURGH!

Just Jason, where are you? Play hide and seek with Jason and find him in each picture.

You've reached the end of this epic adventure! Answer these questions to find out how well you know Just Jason.

1. Just Jason is a part of the:
   a) Cool Crew
   b) No Limits Crew
   c) Extreme Crew

2. Jason's crew has their own:
   a) Channel
   b) Comic book store
   c) TV show

3. Just Jason's favourite gadget is:

a) 

b) 

c) 

4. Just Jason is an amateur:
   a) Singer
   b) Stuntman
   c) Actor

5. Jason's idol is:

a) 

b) 

c) 

ANSWERS

p. 6

p. 7

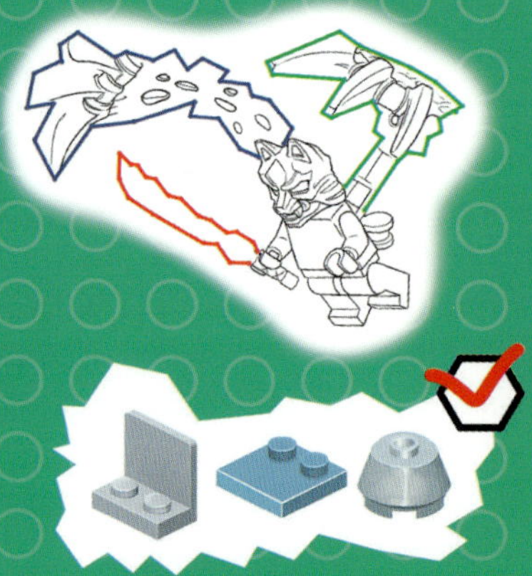

p. 8

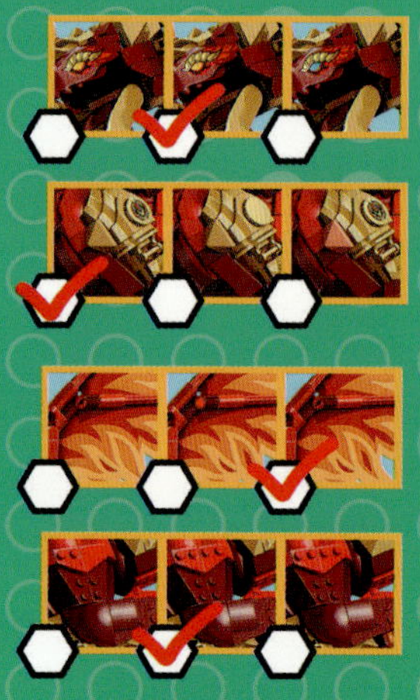

p. 9

p. 12

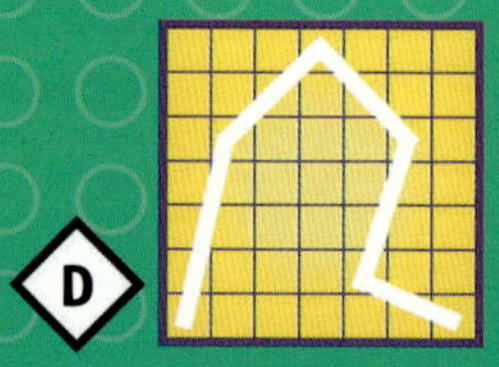

p. 13

p. 14–15

p. 18

p. 19

p. 22

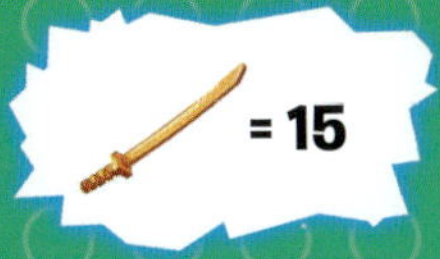

p. 23

p. 24

p. 25

p. 26

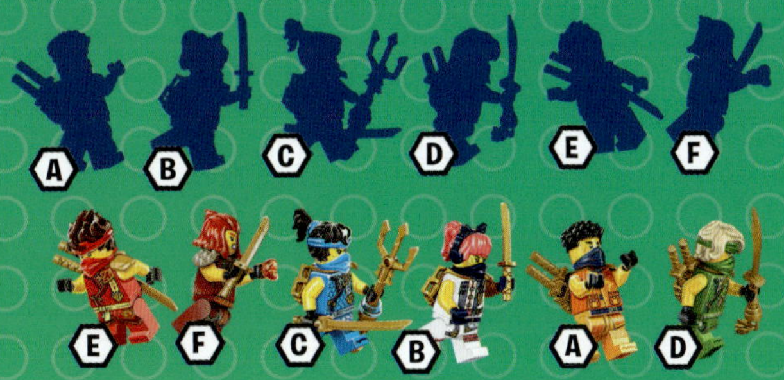

p. 29

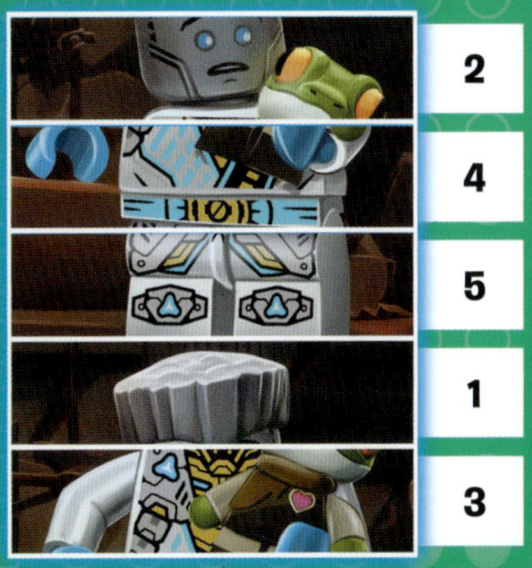

p. 30

p. 31

1. b) 2. c) 3. b)  **4. a) 5. b)**

p. 34

p. 35

p. 38

p. 39

p. 40

p. 41

p. 42

p. 43

p. 44

p. 45

p. 48

p. 49

p. 50

p. 51

p. 52

p. 53

p. 56

p. 57

1. b)
2. a)
3. c) 
4. b)
5. a) 

HOW TO BUILD ZANE

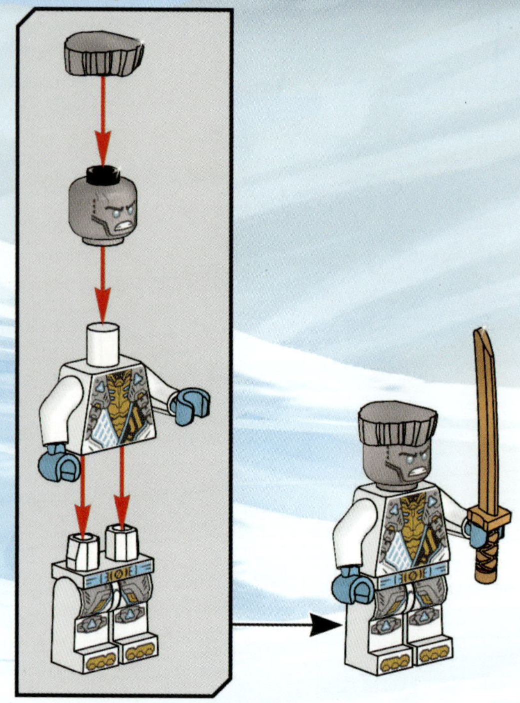